TERMS OF USE

COMPLETE YOUR STUDY KIT

RBT Exam

STUDY WORKBOOK

100-page RBT exam workbook that provides 4 levels of review and learning materials to help you master each item on the task list. Answer key included.

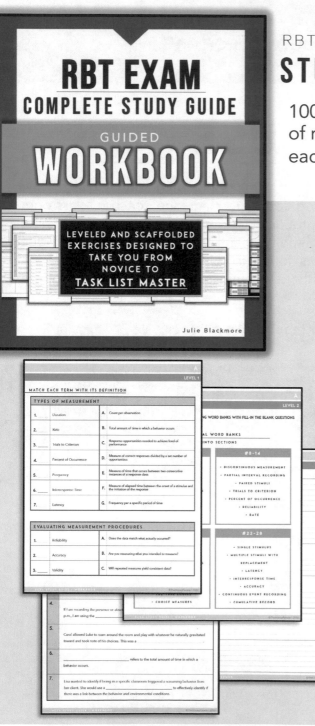

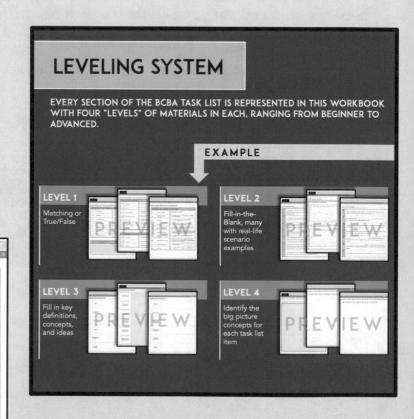

LEVELING SYSTEM

EVERY SECTION OF THE BCBA TASK LIST IS REPRESENTED IN THIS WORKBOOK WITH FOUR "LEVELS" OF MATERIALS IN EACH, RANGING FROM BEGINNER TO ADVANCED.

EXAMPLE

LEVEL 1
Matching or True/False

LEVEL 2
Fill-in-the-Blank, many with real-life scenario examples

LEVEL 3
Fill in key definitions, concepts, and ideas

LEVEL 4
Identify the big picture concepts for each task list item

TABLE OF CONTENTS

INTRODUCTION

The RBT Exam content is based on the **RBT Task List** (also found in this guide). In this study guide, we will explore and define important terms relevant to each section of the RBT Task List.

The Registered Behavior Technician Exam is comprised of **85 multiple-choice questions.**
(10 of which are unscored)

Content Area	Number of Questions
Measurement	12
Assessment	6
Skill Acquisition	24
Behavior Reduction	12
Documentation and Reporting	10
Professional Conduct and Scope of Practice	11
Total	75

Exams are computer-based and administered by Pearson VUE.
The exam must be completed in 90 minutes.

Many questions on the exam are example-based. This means that they will give you a situation and ask you to choose a response that is most appropriate.

This study guide is designed to review the terms, procedures, and assessments that are **crucial to your exam success.**

A. MEASUREMENT

A-1. Prepare for data collection.

A-2. Implement continuous measurement procedures (frequency, duration)

A-3. Implement discontinuous measurement procedures (partial & whole interval, momentary time sampling)

A-4. Implement permanent-product recording procedures.

A-5. Enter data and update graphs.

A-6. Describe behavior and environment in observable and measurable terms.

1. Read data from last session
2. Prepare data sheets and materials based on data from last session.
3. Determine what programs you plan to work on during the session.
4. Gather materials for those programs.
5. Set up the first set of programs so they are ready when you begin the session.

NOTES

A. MEASUREMENT

A-1. Prepare for data collection.

A-2. Implement continuous measurement procedures (frequency, duration)

A-3. Implement discontinuous measurement procedures (partial & whole interval, momentary time sampling)

A-4. Implement permanent-product recording procedures.

A-5. Enter data and update graphs.

A-6. Describe behavior and environment in observable and measurable terms.

Continuous measurement: records every possible behavior occurrence

Frequency: count per observation

Duration: total amount of time in which a behavior occurs

Latency: elapsed time between onset of a stimulus to the initiation of a response

Inter-Response Time (IRT): elapsed time between two successive responses

---

NOTES

A. MEASUREMENT

A-1. Prepare for data collection.

A-2. Implement continuous measurement procedures (frequency, duration)

A-3. **Implement discontinuous measurement procedures (partial & whole interval, momentary time sampling)**

A-4. Implement permanent-product recording procedures.

A-5. Enter data and update graphs.

A-6. Describe behavior and environment in observable and measurable terms.

Discontinuous measurement: records a sample of behavior during an observation

Partial: did the behavior occur at all during the intervention

Whole: did the behavior occur during the whole intervention

Momentary time sampling: is the behavior occurring at this point in time

---

NOTES

A. MEASUREMENT

A-1. Prepare for data collection.

A-2. Implement continuous measurement procedures (frequency, duration)

A-3. Implement discontinuous measurement procedures (partial & whole interval, momentary time sampling)

A-4. Implement permanent-product recording procedures.

A-5. Enter data and update graphs.

A-6. Describe behavior and environment in observable and measurable terms.

Measuring behavior after it occurred by measuring tangible items or the effects a behavior has on an environment.

For example: the number of windows broken, the number of homework problems completed, the number of test questions answered correctly

NOTES

A. MEASUREMENT

A-1. Prepare for data collection.

A-2. Implement continuous measurement procedures (frequency, duration)

A-3. Implement discontinuous measurement procedures (partial & whole interval, momentary time sampling)

A-4. Implement permanent-product recording procedures.

A-5. Enter data and update graphs.

A-6. Describe behavior and environment in observable and measurable terms.

RBTs may assist the BCBA with entering data and updating graphs. Although electronic data may decrease the need for RBT assistance in this area, RBTs should still understand the purpose of data and graphs and also be able to enter data and update graphs as requested by their supervisor.

Data and graphs...

- are important tools in determining effective interventions
- are the collection of all data taken during a session
- are the cornerstone of applied behavior analysis
- can be taken and processed by hand or through computer programs such as Microsoft Excel

NOTES

A. MEASUREMENT

A-1. Prepare for data collection.

A-2. Implement continuous measurement procedures (frequency, duration)

A-3. Implement discontinuous measurement procedures (partial & whole interval, momentary time sampling)

A-4. Implement permanent-product recording procedures.

A-5. Enter data and update graphs.

A-6. Describe behavior and environment in observable and measurable terms.

In order to describe behavior is observable and measurable terms, follow these guidelines:

Behavior is anything a person does that can be observed, repeated, or measured.

Environment is anything that we perceive through the senses.

A good rule of thumb is to always describe a behavior and/or environment so that someone completely unfamiliar with the case would be able to take over data collection just by reading the description.

If I were writing a description of a **tantrum** behavior, these examples show the difference between a *subjective* description and an *observable and measurable* description.

Subjective	Observable and Measurable
Getting extremely worked up and frustrated, yelling or crying	Any incident of kicking legs, throwing self on ground, banging head on floor, crying that lasts at least 1 minute

NOTES

B. ASSESSMENT

B-1. Conduct preference assessments
B-2. Assist with individualized assessment procedures (curriculum-based, developmental, social skills)
B-3. Assist with functional assessment procedures

A **preference assessment** is conducted to identify potential reinforcers. Note, we don't know that these things are actually reinforcing until we see if applying the items increases a behavior. To determine if a potential reinforcer is actually reinforcing, we can do a reinforcer assessment.

Here are some ways to identify a potential reinforcer:

- Ask the learner about their preferences. This is an indirect method. This method can be done by asking open-ended questions, choice format, or rank ordering.
- Pre-task choice- Ask the learner before they work on a task what they would like to "earn" for completing the task. They can choose from 2 to 3 items presented.
- Free operant observation- stay observant and see what the individual gravitates to naturally and plays with in an unrestricted room. The total duration of time that the learner engages with each item or stimulus is recorded. The longer they engage with the stimulus, the stronger the item is preferred.
- Trial-based methods are formal methods to determine potential reinforcers.
  - Single Stimulus (or successful choice method)- a stimulus is presented and the person's reaction to it is noted. This is helpful with individuals who may have trouble choosing between two or more items.
  - Paired Stimuli (or forced choice method)- each trial consists of presenting two items and recording the learner's choice of the two. Data is recorded on how many times an item was chosen and then items are rank ordered. This method takes the most time to implement but is said to be the most accurate.
  - Multiple Stimuli is where many items are presented at one time.
    - Multiple Stimuli with Replacement- the item chosen remains in the array of options and all other items that were not selected are replaced by other items.
    - Multiple Stimuli without Replacement- the item chosen first is taken out of the array and the array diminishes in size on each selection. Second, third, and fourth (etc. choice are recorded in rank order)

B. ASSESSMENT

B-1. Conduct preference assessments

B-2. Assist with individualized assessment procedures (curriculum-based, developmental, social skills)

B-3. Assist with functional assessment procedures

Behavioral and Environmental Assessment- conducting observations of a client's behavior in his/her natural environment. An RBT can provide observations of the client's behavior.

Preference Assessment- determine what items are most preferred by a learner. An RBT can assist with conducting stimulus preference assessments or reinforcer assessments.

Individualized Assessment- curriculum-based, developmental, and/or social skills assessment conducted in interview format.

Functional Assessment- determining cause and effect relationship between environment and behavior. An RBT can assist during Experimental Analysis, collect data during descriptive assessments, or provide information regarding the client.

Probing- asking a learner to perform a task we are unsure they can perform without providing assistance. an RBT can assist by probing new programs to confirm data collected during earlier assessments.

NOTES

B. ASSESSMENT

Functional Assessments- determining cause and effect relationship between environment and behavior and altering either the antecedent or consequence or teaching a replacement behavior.

Functional (Experimental) Analysis- arranging antecedents and consequences so that their separate effect on a problem behavior can be observed and the function can be determined.

Descriptive Assessment- direct observation of behavior under naturally occurring conditions.

Indirect Assessment- using interviews, checklists, rating scales, and questionnaires to obtain information from people familiar with the learner.

NOTES

C. SKILL ACQUISTION

C-1. **Identify the essential components of a written skill acquisition plan.**

C-2. Prepare for the session as required by the skill acquisition plan.

C-3. Use contingencies of reinforcement.

C-4. Implement discrete-trial teaching procedures.

C-5. Implement naturalistic teaching procedures.

C-6. Implement task analyzed chaining procedures.

C-7. Implement discrimination training.

C-8. Implement stimulus control transfer procedures.

C-9. Implement prompt and prompt fading procedures.

C-10. Implement generalization and maintenance procedures.

C-11. Implement shaping procedures.

C-12. Implement token economy procedures.

---

1. Identify skill deficit.
2. Create a goal to address deficit.
3. Identify measurement procedures.
4. Assess current skill level (baseline).
5. Select and implement skill acquisition procedure(s).
6. Take data of target behaviors to determine effectiveness.
7. Modify if necessary to maintain/increase effectiveness.

NOTES

C. SKILL ACQUISTION

C-1. Identify the essential components of a written skill acquisition plan.

C-2. Prepare for the session as required by the skill acquisition plan.

C-3. Use contingencies of reinforcement.

C-4. Implement discrete-trial teaching procedures.

C-5. Implement naturalistic teaching procedures.

C-6. Implement task analyzed chaining procedures.

C-7. Implement discrimination training.

C-8. Implement stimulus control transfer procedures.

C-9. Implement prompt and prompt fading procedures.

C-10. Implement generalization and maintenance procedures.

C-11. Implement shaping procedures.

C-12. Implement token economy procedures.

---

1. Determine what occurred last session to decide where to start.

2. Select skill acquisition procedures to complete during the session.

3. Prepare materials you will need for the skill acquisition procedure (including data collection materials).

NOTES

C. SKILL ACQUISTION

C-1. Identify the essential components of a written skill acquisition plan.

C-2. Prepare for the session as required by the skill acquisition plan.

C-3. Use contingencies of reinforcement.

C-4. Implement discrete-trial teaching procedures.

C-5. Implement naturalistic teaching procedures.

C-6. Implement task analyzed chaining procedures.

C-7. Implement discrimination training.

C-8. Implement stimulus control transfer procedures.

C-9. Implement prompt and prompt fading procedures.

C-10. Implement generalization and maintenance procedures.

C-11. Implement shaping procedures.

C-12. Implement token economy procedures.

Unconditioned reinforcement- inherent and naturally occurring reinforcement, such as food

Conditioned reinforcement- previously neutral stimuli that has become a reinforcer through association with an established reinforcer.

Continuous reinforcement (CRF)- reinforcement is provided for each occurrence of behavior, typically used in the initial stages of learning a new behavior.

Intermittent reinforcement (INT)- some but not all occurrences of a behavior are reinforced, typically used to maintain established behaviors and when progressing toward naturally occurring reinforcement.

Fixed Ratio (FR)- reinforce every n^{th} response.

Variable Ratio (VR)- reinforce roughly every n^{th} response.

Fixed Interval (FI)- reinforce after n amount of time.

Variable Interval (VI)- reinforce roughly after n amount of time.

C. SKILL ACQUISTION

C-1. Identify the essential components of a written skill acquisition plan.

C-2. Prepare for the session as required by the skill acquisition plan.

C-3. Use contingencies of reinforcement.

C-4. Implement discrete-trial teaching procedures.

C-5. Implement naturalistic teaching procedures.

C-6. Implement task analyzed chaining procedures.

C-7. Implement discrimination training.

C-8. Implement stimulus control transfer procedures.

C-9. Implement prompt and prompt fading procedures.

C-10. Implement generalization and maintenance procedures.

C-11. Implement shaping procedures.

C-12. Implement token economy procedures.

Mass trial- asking the target multiple times in a repetitive manner. That would look like this: "Trial 1: Touch dog...Trial 2: Touch dog.....Trial 3: Touch dog". Mass trialing is typically used to teach very young children, children new to ABA, or lower functioning children.

Distractor trial- asking the same target each trial but including two 'unknown" choices as answer options. For example, having a dog card and two cards with objects that are unknown to the learner and saying, "touch dog."

Random Rotation- this is a trial that includes one mastered choice and one trial choice. You would rotate prompts during each trial.

Expanded Trial- similar to the random rotation, but you include *several* mastered choices and only one trial choice. You would rotate prompts with each trial.

Maintenance/Generalization- once a trial choice has been mastered, you would include it in the rotation of mastered choices during random rotation and expanded trials.

C. SKILL ACQUISTION

C-1. Identify the essential components of a written skill acquisition plan.

C-2. Prepare for the session as required by the skill acquisition plan.

C-3. Use contingencies of reinforcement.

C-4. Implement discrete-trial teaching procedures.

C-5. Implement naturalistic teaching procedures.

C-6. Implement task analyzed chaining procedures.

C-7. Implement discrimination training.

C-8. Implement stimulus control transfer procedures.

C-9. Implement prompt and prompt fading procedures.

C-10. Implement generalization and maintenance procedures.

C-11. Implement shaping procedures.

C-12. Implement token economy procedures.

Naturalistic teaching procedures are used to help learners generalize the skills they are learning through their ABA program. You are using the natural environment to generalize learned skills into natural, everyday use.

An example of implementing naturalistic teaching procedures would be to put a desirable item in clear view of a learner to encourage manding.

If a learner can identify and tact a picture of a dog, bringing them in the presence of a real dog and asking, "what is it?" would be another example.

NOTES

C. SKILL ACQUISTION

C-1. Identify the essential components of a written skill acquisition plan.

C-2. Prepare for the session as required by the skill acquisition plan.

C-3. Use contingencies of reinforcement.

C-4. Implement discrete-trial teaching procedures.

C-5. Implement naturalistic teaching procedures.

C-6. Implement task analyzed chaining procedures.

C-7. Implement discrimination training.

C-8. Implement stimulus control transfer procedures.

C-9. Implement prompt and prompt fading procedures.

C-10. Implement generalization and maintenance procedures.

C-11. Implement shaping procedures.

C-12. Implement token economy procedures.

Task analysis- breaking complex skills into smaller, teachable units creating sequential steps.

Forward Chaining- teach the first step of a task, then the second, then the third, until the entire sequence is mastered.

Backward Chaining- Complete a task entirely except for the last step. Teach the learner to complete the last step. Once they have mastered the last step, complete the whole task until the second-to-last step, and then allow them to master that. Continue this process until the entire task is learned.

NOTES

C. SKILL ACQUISTION

C-1. Identify the essential components of a written skill acquisition plan.

C-2. Prepare for the session as required by the skill acquisition plan.

C-3. Use contingencies of reinforcement.

C-4. Implement discrete-trial teaching procedures.

C-5. Implement naturalistic teaching procedures.

C-6. Implement task analyzed chaining procedures.

C-7. Implement discrimination training.

C-8. Implement stimulus control transfer procedures.

C-9. Implement prompt and prompt fading procedures.

C-10. Implement generalization and maintenance procedures.

C-11. Implement shaping procedures.

C-12. Implement token economy procedures.

Discrimination Training- Discrimination training is teaching a client how to tell the difference between two or more stimuli. Reinforcing occurrences of a behavior in the presence of one stimulus condition and not in the presence of another stimulus condition.

Simultaneous- both stimuli are presented at once.

Successive- only one stimulus condition is present.

NOTES

C. SKILL ACQUISTION

C-1. Identify the essential components of a written skill acquisition plan.

C-2. Prepare for the session as required by the skill acquisition plan.

C-3. Use contingencies of reinforcement.

C-4. Implement discrete-trial teaching procedures.

C-5. Implement naturalistic teaching procedures.

C-6. Implement task analyzed chaining procedures.

C-7. Implement discrimination training.

C-8. Implement stimulus control transfer procedures.

C-9. Implement prompt and prompt fading procedures.

C-10. Implement generalization and maintenance procedures.

C-11. Implement shaping procedures.

C-12. Implement token economy procedures.

Stimulus control transfer procedures are techniques in which prompts are discontinued once the target behavior is being displayed in the presence of the discriminative stimulus (Sd). Prompt fading and prompt delay are used in stimulus control transfer procedures.

Example:

RBT: "Say cup"

Learner: "Cup"

RBT: Points to a picture of a cup

Learner: "Cup"

NOTES

C. SKILL ACQUISTION

C-1. Identify the essential components of a written skill acquisition plan.

C-2. Prepare for the session as required by the skill acquisition plan.

C-3. Use contingencies of reinforcement.

C-4. Implement discrete-trial teaching procedures.

C-5. Implement naturalistic teaching procedures.

C-6. Implement task analyzed chaining procedures.

C-7. Implement discrimination training.

C-8. Implement stimulus control transfer procedures.

C-9. Implement prompt and prompt fading procedures.

C-10. Implement generalization and maintenance procedures.

C-11. Implement shaping procedures.

C-12. Implement token economy procedures.

Prompt fading- there are two methods to fade a prompt.

- **Most to least-** With this method you start the most intrusive prompts and gradually fade to less intrusive prompts. You might follow a prompting hierarchy such as: <u>Full physical</u>, <u>partial physical</u>, <u>model</u>, <u>verbal</u>, <u>gestural</u>, <u>independent</u>.

- **Least to most:** The method involves starting with the least intrusive prompts and moving up in the prompting hierarchy. This can be beneficial because it gives students to the opportunity to be independent and you are only providing as much prompting as needed. This is a strategy we tend to use naturally. Once you introduce a task, allow wait time to see how they respond naturally. Then you can give a gestural prompt. If this doesn't produce a correct response, move up to a verbal, and so on.

NOTES

C. SKILL ACQUISTION

C-1. Identify the essential components of a written skill acquisition plan.

C-2. Prepare for the session as required by the skill acquisition plan.

C-3. Use contingencies of reinforcement.

C-4. Implement discrete-trial teaching procedures.

C-5. Implement naturalistic teaching procedures.

C-6. Implement task analyzed chaining procedures.

C-7. Implement discrimination training.

C-8. Implement stimulus control transfer procedures.

C-9. Implement prompt and prompt fading procedures.

C-10. Implement generalization and maintenance procedures.

C-11. Implement shaping procedures.

C-12. Implement token economy procedures.

Generalization- teach learned targets in the natural environment

Examples:

- teach the word car with many different pictures of different cars

- having two people teach the same skill

Maintenance- including mastered item or skill into programs

Examples:

- discrete trials using random rotation or extended trials

NOTES

C. SKILL ACQUISTION

C-1. Identify the essential components of a written skill acquisition plan.

C-2. Prepare for the session as required by the skill acquisition plan.

C-3. Use contingencies of reinforcement.

C-4. Implement discrete-trial teaching procedures.

C-5. Implement naturalistic teaching procedures.

C-6. Implement task analyzed chaining procedures.

C-7. Implement discrimination training.

C-8. Implement stimulus control transfer procedures.

C-9. Implement prompt and prompt fading procedures.

C-10. Implement generalization and maintenance procedures.

C-11. Implement shaping procedures.

C-12. Implement token economy procedures.

Shaping is the process of teaching a new behavior gradually by rewarding behaviors that progressively come close to the target behavior. An example of shaping could be:

Target behavior: Jane to complete a full 10-question homework assignment. After probing, she has not been successful in completing the task independently.

1. Require Jane to turn in a paper with just her name on it. Reward with reinforcement.
2. Require Jane to turn in a paper with one question completed. Provide reinforcement.
3. Require Jane to turn in a paper with two questions completed. Provide reinforcement.

You would continue this process until the child has met the target behavior. This is only one example of shaping, and the method of shaping can be used in many different ways.

NOTES

C. SKILL ACQUISTION

C-1. Identify the essential components of a written skill acquisition plan.

C-2. Prepare for the session as required by the skill acquisition plan.

C-3. Use contingencies of reinforcement.

C-4. Implement discrete-trial teaching procedures.

C-5. Implement naturalistic teaching procedures.

C-6. Implement task analyzed chaining procedures.

C-7. Implement discrimination training.

C-8. Implement stimulus control transfer procedures.

C-9. Implement prompt and prompt fading procedures.

C-10. Implement generalization and maintenance procedures.

C-11. Implement shaping procedures.

C-12. Implement token economy procedures.

A token economy is a system of generalized conditioned reinforcers.

The individual who receives the generalized tokens can save them and exchange for a variety of backup reinforcers.

Basically, an individual earns generalized reinforcers (stickers, points, *tokens*) which can be exchanged for an actual reward (i.e., break, game, toy, snack).

Conditioned reinforcer- A stimulus that acquired its reinforcing value by being paired with other reinforcers. Conditioned reinforcers are also called secondary reinforcers or learned reinforcers and required pairing to understand their value and be positive for "me". Such as social, hugs, tickles, activities, etc.

Backup reinforcer- The reinforcer that is paired with a conditioned reinforcer or a generalized conditioned reinforcer.

An example might be:

Jamie loves to watch Barney videos

She earns tokens on a board for staying seated on the carpet during story time

After earning a predetermined number of tokens, she exchanges them for access to Barney videos

D. BEHAVIOR REDUCTION

D-1. Identify essential components of a written behavior reduction plan.

D-2. Describe common functions of behavior.

D-3. Implement interventions based on modification of antecedents such as motivating operations and discriminative stimuli.

D-4. Implement differential reinforcement procedures (e.g. DRA, DRO).

D-5. Implement extinction procedures.

D-6. Implement crisis/emergency procedures according to protocol.

A **behavior plan** is useful because it helps the behavior technician address behaviors effectively. Typically, the Behavior Analyst will develop the behavior plan and the RBT will implement it during ABA sessions.

A written behavior plan must include the following:

- Operational definitions of target behaviors
- Antecedent modifications
- Replacement behaviors
- Consequence modifications
- Persons responsible
- Emergency measures
- Function of behavior

NOTES

D. BEHAVIOR REDUCTION

D-1. Identify essential components of a written behavior reduction plan.

D-2. Describe common functions of behavior.

D-3. Implement interventions based on modification of antecedents such as motivating operations and discriminative stimuli.

D-4. Implement differential reinforcement procedures (e.g. DRA, DRO).

D-5. Implement extinction procedures.

D-6. Implement crisis/emergency procedures according to protocol.

The four functions of behavior are important to remember when providing ABA services. All behaviors are maintained by one or more of the four functions of behavior.

The four functions of behavior include:

- **Attention**
  - Example: A child whines to get his mom to come play with him.
- **Access to Tangibles**
  - Example: A child grabs a toy out of his classmate's hand because he wanted it.
- **Escape**
  - Example: A child tears up a math worksheet so he will not have to complete it.
- **Automatic Reinforcement**
  - Example: Picking at scabs so much that they bleed, excessive rocking or noise-making

NOTES

D. BEHAVIOR REFERENCE

Antecedents refer to things that occur before the identified behavior or skill.

Modifying antecedents refers to making changes in the client's environment prior to the client working on a specific skill or displaying a specific behavior. For instance, when looking at behavior reduction, modifying antecedents would involve making changes that will help decrease the likelihood that the behavior will occur.

Antecedent strategies are a good strategy for teachers and caregivers/parents alike. This is because you are able to use these strategies to prevent the problem behavior from happening rather than waiting until the problem behavior occurs and then trying to react effectively.

Motivating operations refers to a behavior concept which identifies the degree to which the learner will be reinforced by the consequences of their behavior. For example, if a child is really hungry, they may be more likely to complete a task and be reinforced by the reward of a snack.

An **establishing operation** increases the effectiveness of a reinforcer. For example, if a child has not played video games all day (but loves them), he may be more likely to complete his chores and homework (or complete therapy tasks in an ABA session) to earn the video game.

Discriminative stimuli, also known as SDs, are the stimuli that are used to elicit a specific response. For example, showing a child an ice-cream cone and saying, "What is this?", may elicit the child in saying, "Ice-cream."

D. BEHAVIOR REDUCTION

D-1. Identify essential components of a written behavior reduction plan.

D-2. Describe common functions of behavior.

D-3. Implement interventions based on modification of antecedents such as motivating operations and discriminative stimuli.

D-4. Implement differential reinforcement procedures (e.g. DRA, DRO).

D-5. Implement extinction procedures.

D-6. Implement crisis/emergency procedures according to protocol.

DRI - Differential Reinforcement of Incompatible Behavior

This procedures entails only reinforcing behaviors that are incompatible with the problem behavior while withholding reinforcement for the problem behavior. In other words, only behaviors that cannot occur simultaneously with the problem behavior are reinforced.

Example: Kevin engages in out of seat behavior, so his teacher decides to implement a DRI procedure. She decides to reinforce a behavior that is incompatible with out of seat behavior. Sitting in his seat is chosen as the incompatible behavior because it cannot occur at the same time as out of seat behavior. Kevin only receives reinforcement (ex. token) for sitting in his seat while reinforcement is withheld when Kevin is out of his seat.

DRA - Differential Reinforcement of Alternate Behavior

This procedure entails reinforcing a behavior that serves as a viable alternative for the problem behavior but is not necessarily incompatible with the problem behavior.

Example: Sarah engages in shouting out behavior after her teacher poses a question to the class. Her teacher decides to use a DRA procedure in which Sarah is only reinforced (ex. called on) for raising her hand to answer a question. This behavior is an alternative to shouting out but is not incompatible as both the problem behavior and the alternative can occur at the same time. However, raising her hand is a more socially acceptable alternative.

DRO - Differential Reinforcement of Other Behavior

This procedure entails delivering reinforcement whenever the problem behavior does not occur during a predetermined amount of time.

Example: Julie pulls strands of hair out of her head when she is completing independent work. Her teacher decides to use DRO in order to reinforce the absence of pulling her hair. Using this procedure, the teacher sets a timer for three minutes on Julie's desk. If Julie does not pull her hair for the entire three minutes, then she is reinforced. If Julie does pull her hair, she is not reinforced, and the timer is reset.

DRL - Differential Reinforcement of Low Rates

This procedure is used to reduce the frequency of a behavior but not eliminate it from the learner's repertoire entirely. This is typically reserved for behaviors that are socially acceptable but may occur too often. Using this procedure, reinforcement is delivered if a behavior occurs below a predetermined criteria.

Example: James uses socially appropriate behavior to greet peers but does so up to ten times in one class period. His teacher decides to use DRL to lower the rate of his behavior, but she does not want to eliminate it completely. She decides to deliver reinforcement (ex. computer time) to James if he greets peers five or fewer times during the class period. If he greets peers more than five times, he does not receive reinforcement.

D. BEHAVIOR REDUCTION

D-1. Identify essential components of a written behavior reduction plan.

D-2. Describe common functions of behavior.

D-3. Implement interventions based on modification of antecedents such as motivating operations and discriminative stimuli.

D-4. Implement differential reinforcement procedures (e.g. DRA, DRO).

D-5. Implement extinction procedures.

D-6. Implement crisis/emergency procedures according to protocol.

Extinction refers to the ABA principle of no longer providing reinforcement to a previously reinforced behavior. Basically, when the reinforcement for a behavior stops, the behavior will likely stop, as well.

In clinical practice, ABA providers sometimes associate ignoring the child or ignoring the behavior with extinction. However, this is not truly the way extinction works.

Extinction involves no longer providing the reinforcement for a behavior. The reinforcement may have been attention in which case ignoring the behavior may be acceptable as an extinction procedure. However, when the reinforcement of the behavior is actually escape rather than attention, ignoring is not necessarily a true form of extinction. When a behavior is maintained by the function of escape, extinction would include no longer allowing escape from the demand.

NOTES

D. BEHAVIOR REDUCTION

D-1. Identify essential components of a written behavior reduction plan.

D-2. Describe common functions of behavior.

D-3. Implement interventions based on modification of antecedents such as motivating operations and discriminative stimuli.

D-4. Implement differential reinforcement procedures (e.g. DRA, DRO).

D-5. Implement extinction procedures.

D-6. Implement crisis/emergency procedures according to protocol.

The setting in which an RBT works will dictate what crisis or emergency procedures will be used in an ABA session. However, there are some general procedures that should be considered.

It is important to have a plan for how you as the RBT will address any maladaptive behaviors especially behaviors that could pose a danger to the client or anyone else. Typically, a supervisor or Behavior Analyst will be able to assist in developing this plan.

Also, it is important to understand laws regarding mandated reporting of child abuse and neglect, how to report any concerning incidents that may occur, and what to do about illness or injury. An RBT should have first aid knowledge and have emergency contact information to be used during their session (including contact information for local emergency services such as the fire and police departments as well as emergency contacts for the client specifically).

NOTES

E. DOCUMENTATION AND REPORTING

E-1. Effectively communicate with a supervisor in an ongoing manner.

E-2. Actively seek clinical direction from supervisor in a timely manner.

E-3. Report other variables that might affect the client in a timely manner.

E-4. Generate objective session notes for service verification by describing what occurred during the sessions, in accordance with applicable legal, regulatory, and workplace requirements.

E-5. Comply with applicable legal, regulatory, and workplace data collection, storage, transportation, and documentation requirements.

- Engaging in regular communication with your clinical team.

- Taking an active role in effectively communicating all aspects of your daily interactions with your clients and caregivers.

- Understanding boundaries in relation to your supervisor's time and responsibilities (knowing when it is appropriate to talk with your supervisor and when you should allow your supervisor time to observe, analyze data, or complete other tasks).

- Knowing what situations should result in immediate or more urgent communication with your supervisor and knowing what situations can wait until your supervisor attends session for observation or has a meeting with you to discuss the case or client.

- Speaking respectfully and professionally.

- Accepting feedback and responding appropriately to feedback and communication from your supervisor.

- Expressing ideas and professional opinions with healthy assertiveness while also understanding your role in complying with your supervisor's treatment planning.

Your supervisor will check-in on you on a regular basis; if this is not occurring, you are encouraged to contact the C.A.B.A. office directly and ask to speak to a senior clinical team member

NOTES

E. DOCUMENTATION AND REPORTING

E-1. Effectively communicate with a supervisor in an ongoing manner.

E-2. Actively seek clinical direction from supervisor in a timely manner.

E-3. Report other variables that might affect the client in a timely manner.

E-4. Generate objective session notes for service verification by describing what occurred during the sessions, in accordance with applicable legal, regulatory, and workplace requirements.

E-5. Comply with applicable legal, regulatory, and workplace data collection, storage, transportation, and documentation requirements.

It is your responsibility as a Registered Behavior Technician to seek out guidance and direction from your supervisor(s) when needed. If you are unsure of protocol or steps you should be taking in a wide range of scenarios regarding your clients, you must contact a supervisor in a timely manner in order to achieve clear guidance before your next session (in most cases). You can, and should, request overlap sessions in which you can receive in-person supervision as well.

NOTES

E. DOCUMENTATION AND REPORTING

E-1. Effectively communicate with a supervisor in an ongoing manner.

E-2. Actively seek clinical direction from supervisor in a timely manner.

E-3. Report other variables that might affect the client in a timely manner.

E-4. Generate objective session notes for service verification by describing what occurred during the sessions, in accordance with applicable legal, regulatory, and workplace requirements.

E-5. Comply with applicable legal, regulatory, and workplace data collection, storage, transportation, and documentation requirements.

There are many factors that an RBT or other ABA service provider should consider regarding a client's functioning. In the field of applied behavior analysis, setting events are sometimes neglected to be considered as influencers of behavior. Setting events are in a way broader experiences that a client may have. While antecedents could be seen as the trigger for a behavior or as the thing that happens right before a behavior occurs, a setting event is a larger situational experience.

Some examples of setting events include:

- Illness
- Lack of sleep
- Biological needs (like hunger)
- Changes in the client's home environment

Setting events make it more likely that a specific behavior will occur. For example, if a toddler has a lack of quality sleep, they may be more likely to tantrum as a result of another child taking a toy away rather than if they had a good night's sleep. When the toddler has slept well, maybe they are more likely to share rather than tantrum in response to other youth trying to play with the toys they were interacting with.

E. DOCUMENTATION AND REPORTING

E-1. Effectively communicate with a supervisor in an ongoing manner.

E-2. Actively seek clinical direction from supervisor in a timely manner.

E-3. Report other variables that might affect the client in a timely manner.

E-4. Generate objective session notes for service verification by describing what occurred during the sessions, in accordance with applicable legal, regulatory, and workplace requirements.

E-5. Comply with applicable legal, regulatory, and workplace data collection, storage, transportation, and documentation requirements.

It is important to complete session notes objectively and professionally. Objective refers to disclosing only facts and actual information or observations. This is in contrast to subjective information which includes adding your own personal thoughts and feelings into your session notes.

When RBTs complete session notes, they should remember that the note will be included in that client's permanent record and therefore the note should be accurate and professionally written. In a session note you could also mention the setting events or factors that may have influenced the client's behaviors throughout session. However, be sure to only use objective information and not to assume that you know why the child acted the way they did. For example, you may mention that the client's parent reported at the beginning of session that the client only slept five hours last night and that he had a fever last week.

Remember that it is important to generate objective session notes also so that others (such as other RBTs that may work with your client or your supervisor who oversees treatment planning) can be aware of what occurred during the session.

NOTES

E. DOCUMENTATION AND REPORTING

E-1. Effectively communicate with a supervisor in an ongoing manner.

E-2. Actively seek clinical direction from supervisor in a timely manner.

E-3. Report other variables that might affect the client in a timely manner.

E-4. Generate objective session notes for service verification by describing what occurred during the sessions, in accordance with applicable legal, regulatory, and workplace requirements.

E-5. Comply with applicable legal, regulatory, and workplace data collection, storage, transportation, and documentation requirements.

There are laws and regulations regarding how to handle paperwork including data collection and documents specifically as it relates to how to store them and how to travel with them.

If you provide home-based services, it is imperative that you be careful when travelling with client documentation. Be mindful of confidentiality laws. Carry as little client data and documents as you need while you travel. Whatever you do travel with should be carefully stored such as by locking it in a travel briefcase and possibly even in your truck (think of it as locking the data twice – once in the briefcase and once in the trunk). However, again, this is not to be taken as legal advice. You should speak to a supervisor or knowledgeable person in your area to learn about the specific regulations related to your location and workplace setting.

In the United States, you must comply with all HIPAA policies and regulations. HIPAA requires that a client's data and paperwork and identifying information be kept confidential and protected. You should store client data sheets, session notes, and paperwork in a secure location. You should always put them back after a session so that they are kept in that safe location.

NOTES

F. PROFESSIONAL CONDUCT AND SCOPE OF PRACTICE

F-1. Describe the BACB's RBT supervision requirements and the role of RBTs in the service-delivery system.

F-2. Respond appropriately to feedback and maintain or improve performance accordingly.

F-3. Communicate with stakeholders as authorized.

F-4. Maintain professional boundaries.

F-5. Maintain client dignity.

The RBT's role involves implementing the service protocol designed by the supervisor which could be any of the other three credentials (including the BCaBA, BCBA, or BCBA-D). A BCaBA requires oversight by a BCBA or BCBA-D.

An RBT is the credential at a high school diploma level. The BCaBA is a bachelor's degree level credential and is known as an Assistant Behavior Analyst. The BCBA is a master's level degree credential. Individuals with this credential are known as Behavior Analysts. The BCBA-D credential is a doctoral level position. BCBA-D's are also known as Behavior Analysts.

The RBT is required to provide the direct ABA service to the identified client including skill acquisition programs and behavior intervention plans.

The BACB presents a tiered service delivery model for the provision of behavior analysis services. In this model of service delivery, there are two possible organizational strategies. One includes multiple RBTs working under the direction of a BCBA or BCBA-D. The second one includes multiple RBTs working under the direction of a BCaBA while one or more BCaBAs can work under the direction of a BCBA or BCBA-D.

It is important to understand that the supervisor (BCBA-D, BCBA, or BCaBA) develops the treatment plans, makes modifications to treatment, and provides a majority of clinical recommendations to caregivers and other professionals while the RBT implements the service plans to the client and assists with some of the supervisory activities.

F. PROFESSIONAL CONDUCT AND SCOPE OF PRACTICE

F-1. Describe the BACB's RBT supervision requirements and the role of RBTs in the service-delivery system.

F-2. Respond appropriately to feedback and maintain or improve performance accordingly.

F-3. Communicate with stakeholders as authorized.

F-4. Maintain professional boundaries.

F-5. Maintain client dignity.

Responding appropriately to feedback and maintaining or improving performance accordingly is an important skill of RBTs. Part of an RBTs role includes taking feedback from a supervisor. The supervisor will be modifying treatment to help ensure the client is making progress on goals and to help with any behavioral concerns that arise.

To respond appropriately to feedback, the RBT should utilize active listening skills which involves listening to and comprehending what information the supervisor provides. An RBT should utilize the following tips in response to feedback:

- Act professionally and respectfully
- Implement changes recommended by the supervisor
- Bring concerns to the supervisor in a clear and timely manner yet still understanding the supervisor's role is to make the final decision in the treatment plan
- Be consistent with the implementation of the feedback provided throughout treatment sessions
- Document treatment modifications appropriately

NOTES

F. PROFESSIONAL CONDUCT AND SCOPE OF PRACTICE

F-1. Describe the BACB's RBT supervision requirements and the role of RBTs in the service-delivery system.

F-2. Respond appropriately to feedback and maintain or improve performance accordingly.

F-3. Communicate with stakeholders as authorized.

F-4. Maintain professional boundaries.

F-5. Maintain client dignity.

A Registered Behavior Technician's primary task is to implement ABA intervention as designed by their supervisor (typically a BCBA or BCaBA).

RBTs do not often provide formal communication with stakeholders. However, any communication that takes place must be respectful and professional in nature. Sometimes an RBT may participate in team meetings with the client's caregiver and sometimes other professionals, such as teachers or other service providers like speech therapists or occupational therapists.

As an RBT, it is important to remember that your supervisor should be making all clinical decisions regarding the case you are working on. An RBT should support the supervisor and direct any questions or concerns from the caregiver to the supervisor for further assistance above what the RBT has already been trained to respond to. In a school meeting (such as for an IEP-Individualized Education Plan meeting), an RBT may participate to give their input as to the status of ABA services, but all decisions and recommendations should come from the supervisor.

RBTs should display respectful and professional communication at all times.

NOTES

F. PROFESSIONAL CONDUCT AND SCOPE OF PRACTICE

F-1. Describe the BACB's RBT supervision requirements and the role of RBTs in the service-delivery system.

F-2. Respond appropriately to feedback and maintain or improve performance accordingly.

F-3. Communicate with stakeholders as authorized.

F-4. Maintain professional boundaries.

F-5. Maintain client dignity.

It is essential to maintain professional boundaries in any human service position.

However, as an RBT, you may become attached to your client due to the intensity and involvement you have with the family.

However, it is important to always remember what your role is and that you are providing a professional service.

Do not develop any relationship outside the professional service provider – client relationship.

To avoid dual relationships or conflicts of interest, be sure to keep conversation to professional topics.

Do not speak very in depth about any personal issues (no more than enough to maintain a friendly, professional manner).

If possible, do not provide clients or caregivers your personal phone number.

If you personally know a potential client, it is important to avoid working with that individual if possible.

Sometimes in rural communities, extra steps may be necessary to establish professional boundaries. Do not have contact with clients or their relatives on social media.

This is important to help maintain the professional boundaries of the service provider – client relationship.

F. PROFESSIONAL CONDUCT AND SCOPE OF PRACTICE

F-1. Describe the BACB's RBT supervision requirements and the role of RBTs in the service-delivery system.

F-2. Respond appropriately to feedback and maintain or improve performance accordingly.

F-3. Communicate with stakeholders as authorized.

F-4. Maintain professional boundaries.

F-5. Maintain client dignity.

Dignity refers to "the state or quality of being worthy of honor or respect." All people have the right to dignity and respect. Dignity is not something that people have to earn. You can maintain a client's dignity by showing respect at all times, maintaining privacy and confidentiality, and communicating effectively and professionally.

- Do not talk down to your clients or belittle them.

- Always treat your client as a human and not just a number or a problem.

- Don't speak to your clients in non-professional ways such as by being overly friendly or overly aggressive.

- Make sure that your personal views and judgments do not interfere with providing quality treatment or create a problem with maintaining client dignity.

  - For example, if you personally have an issue with parents who smoke and you are working with a client who has a mother who smokes often, don't allow your personal views to interfere with how you treat that client and his family.

- Avoid having side conversations (or small talk) with coworkers when you are supposed to be focusing on your client (which should be at all times during the time you are providing a service).

- Be compassionate and empathetic toward your clients.

  - This means that you should act in ways that show you are aware of your client's feelings and experiences and that you are understanding of their situation and are truly trying to help them.

- The area of professional conduct requires that RBTs act in ways that are respectful and considerate of their clients.

- Communicating with stakeholders must be done in an appropriate manner.

- You should only communicate with stakeholders in ways that you, as the RBT, have been directed to.

Maintaining professional boundaries and client dignity is an essential part of providing quality ABA services.

RBT TASK LIST (2ND ED.)

The BACB's Registered Behavior Technician Task List includes the primary tasks that are likely to be performed by behavior technicians with some, but not necessarily all, clients. It is at the discretion of an RBT supervisor to determine any activities outside of this task list that a behavior technician is competent to perform as a behavior technician.

The RBT Task List content serves as the basis for the RBT training requirement and the RBT examination. The Task List is organized into the following primary content areas: <u>Measurement</u>, <u>Assessment</u>, <u>Skill Acquisition</u>, <u>Behavior Reduction</u>, <u>Documentation and Reporting</u>, and <u>Professional Conduct and Scope of Practice</u>.

A. MEASUREMENT

A-1. Prepare for data collection.

A-2. Implement continuous measurement procedures (e.g., frequency, duration).

A-3. Implement discontinuous measurement procedures (partial & whole interval, momentary time sampling).

A-4. Implement permanent-product recording procedures.

A-5. Enter data and update graphs.

A-6. Describe behavior and environment in observable and measurable terms.

B. ASSESSMENT

B-1. Conduct preference assessments.

B-2. Assist with individualized assessment procedures (curriculum-based, developmental, social skills).

B-3. Assist with functional assessment procedures.

C. SKILL ACQUISTION

C-1. Identify the essential components of a written skill acquisition plan.

C-2. Prepare for the session as required by the skill acquisition plan.

C-3. Use contingencies of reinforcement (e.g., conditioned/unconditioned reinforcement, continuous/intermittent schedules).

C-4. Implement discrete-trial teaching procedures.

C-5. Implement naturalistic teaching procedures (e.g., incidental).

C-6. Implement task analyzed chaining procedures.

C-7. Implement discrimination training.

C-8. Implement stimulus control transfer procedures.

C-9. Implement prompt and prompt fading procedures.

C-10. Implement generalization and maintenance procedures.

C-11. Implement shaping procedures.

C-12. Implement token economy procedures.

RBT TASK LIST (2ND ED.)

D. BEHAVIOR REDUCTION

D-1. Identify essential components of a written behavior reduction plan.

D-2. Describe common functions of behavior.

D-3. Implement interventions based on modification of antecedents such as motivating operations and discriminative stimuli.

D-4. Implement differential reinforcement procedures (e.g., DRA, DRO).

D-5. Implement extinction procedures.

D-6. Implement crisis/emergency procedures according to protocol.

E. DOCUMENTATION AND REPORTING

E-1. Effectively communicate with a supervisor in an ongoing manner.

E-2. Actively seek clinical direction from supervisor in a timely manner.

E-3. Report other variables that might affect the client in a timely manner.

E-4. Generate objective session notes for service verification by describing what occurred during the sessions, in accordance with applicable legal, regulatory, and workplace requirements.

E-5. Comply with applicable legal, regulatory, and workplace data collection, storage, transportation, and documentation requirements.

F. PROFESSIONAL CONDUCT AND SCOPE OF PRACTICE

F-1. Describe the BACB's RBT supervision requirements and the role of RBTs in the service-delivery system.

F-2. Respond appropriately to feedback and maintain or improve performance accordingly.

F-3. Communicate with stakeholders (e.g., family, caregivers, other professionals) as authorized.

F-4. Maintain professional boundaries (e.g., avoid dual relationships, conflicts of interest, social media contacts).

F-5. Maintain client dignity.

WHY BECOME AN RBT?

There are so many advantages to earning the certification of **Registered Behavior Technician**. As an RBT, many times you will be referred to as an ABA therapist. Although you do not hold a degree in therapy, you will be providing ABA therapy.

What exactly is an ABA therapist?

It's important to distinguish between an ABA Therapist and a Behavior Analyst. Behavior Analysts supervise, manage, and run ABA programs as consultants. ABA Therapists are the foundation of any ABA program, as they are the ones who work with the consumer day after day to teach skills. As an ABA Therapist you are usually responsible for teaching very specific skills and implementing a behavior plan written by a BCBA. ABA therapists can also work with a variety of clients, not just young kids with autism. There's a growing demand from schools who want ABA services for typically developing children, as well as ABA professionals working with adult populations and animals.

What is it like being an ABA therapist?

The clients you work with can take you from sheer joy to the pit of frustration very quickly! On Monday your client could be excited to see you and give you a huge hug, and then on Thursday they might try to bite you. Even if you only work with one client, every day won't be the same. That's what is so great about this job; if you have a bad session you get to hit "reset" and start over again the next day. If you are a person who loves sameness, routine, and predictability, you might not enjoy this type of work. The field changes all of the time, parent expectations can change, the behavior plan can change, the programs change. Being happy with change is pretty important!

What kind of person would be a goof fit as an RBT / ABA therapist?

Anyone who is passionate about special needs or human differences, detail oriented, energetic, and loves to learn. Parents often feed off of the enthusiasm of the ABA Therapist and feel encouraged by it. It's important that as an ABA professional you enjoy learning, because you never stop learning when this is your job. Research and technology advance the field regularly. You have to be open to receiving supervision and correction, even if you have been doing this for years. If you aren't a person who can take constructive criticism, then this likely isn't the job for you!

What are the hours like?

There's a lot of variability as far as scheduling, and of course depending on your work setting. If you work inside of homes with very young children, you'll probably have early morning hours (as most young children still nap). If you work at a school, then most likely you will have an 8-3 schedule. If you work for an agency, you will likely have a jam-packed schedule of varying days and times, sometimes with really unpleasant huge gaps in your schedule. Example: Monday sessions at 9-12 and 4-7. **Working weekends should not be mandatory.** If you burn yourself out with a hectic caseload then what do you have left to give to your clients, or to yourself and your own family?

Do I *have* to have an RBT credential?

The Registered Behavior Technician (RBT) credential is fairly new in the field and is a means to establish a minimum education and training requirement for ABA Technicians. Is it necessary to enter the field/get a job? No. *But...* employers may require it, funding sources may require it, and it is a great way to learn more about the science of behavior analysis. Keep in mind the RBT professional is not intended as a standalone position. Meaning, you cannot work independently as a RBT -- you will need a supervising BCBA.

Where can I find RBT jobs?

This can be tricky. It's often easier to find an ABA job when you already have one, because of referrals/word of mouth. If you are looking to break into the field, I'd recommend working for an ABA provider/agency first. You will get more clients and supervision than you would striking out on your own. Research the ABA providers in your area and contact them to see if they need ABA therapists. If they don't hire inexperienced therapists, see if they have volunteer positions so you can gain experience. Try to obtain the RBT credential on your own, as it makes you a competitive job seeker even if you lack experience. You can also try your local or state organizations for ABA, as they often allow members to post job openings on their website. If you are currently a college student, often the heads of the Education or Psychology departments will have leads on ABA jobs/practicum sites.

A. MEASUREMENT

A-1. Prepare for data collection.

1. Read data from last session

2. Prepare data sheets and materials based on data from last session.

3. Determine what programs you plan to work on during the session.

4. Gather materials for those programs.

5. Set up the first set of programs so they are ready when you begin the session.

A-2. Implement continuous measurement procedure

Continuous measurement: records every possible behavior occurrence

Frequency: count per observation

Duration: total amount of time in which a behavior occurs

Latency: elapsed time between onset of a stimulus to the initiation of a response

Inter-Response Time (IRT): elapsed time between two successive responses

A-3. Implement discontinuous measurement procedures

Discontinuous measurement: records a sample of behavior during an observation

Partial: did the behavior occur at all during the intervention

Whole: did the behavior occur during the whole intervention

Momentary time sampling: is the behavior occurring at this point in time

A-4. Implement permanent-product recording procedures.

Measuring behavior after it occurred by measuring tangible items or the effects a behavior has on an environment.

For example: the number of windows broken, the number of homework problems completed, the number of test questions answered correctly

A-5. Enter data and update graphs.

RBTs may assist the BCBA with entering data and updating graphs. Although electronic data may decrease the need for RBT assistance in this area, RBTs should still understand the purpose of data and graphs and also be able to enter data and update graphs as requested by their supervisor.

Data and graphs...
- are important tools in determining effective interventions
- are the collection of all data taken during a session
- are the cornerstone of applied behavior analysis
- can be taken and processed by hand or through computer programs such as Microsoft Excel

A-6. Describe behavior and environment in observable and measurable terms.

In order to describe behavior is observable and measurable terms, follow these guidelines:

Behavior is anything a person does that can be observed, repeated, or measured.

Environment is anything that we perceive through the senses.

A good rule of thumb is to always describe a behavior and/or environment so that someone completely unfamiliar with the case would be able to take over data collection just by reading the description.

B. ASSESSMENT

B-1. Conduct preference assessments

A **preference assessment** is conducted to identify potential reinforcers. Note, we don't know that these things are actually reinforcing until we see if applying the items increases a behavior. To determine if a potential reinforcer is actually reinforcing, we can do a reinforcer assessment.

Types of Preference Assessments: (see study guide for more in-depth descriptions)

- Pre-task choice
- Free operant observation
- Single Stimulus
- Paired Stimulus
- Multiple Stimuli with Replacement
- Multiple Stimuli without Replacement

B-2. Assist with individualized assessment procedures

Behavioral and Environmental Assessment- conducting observations of a client's behavior in his/her natural environment. An RBT can provide observations of the client's behavior.

Preference Assessment- determine what items are most preferred by a learner. An RBT can assist with conducting stimulus preference assessments or reinforcer assessments.

Individualized Assessment- curriculum-based, developmental, and/or social skills assessment conducted in interview format.

Functional Assessment- determining cause and effect relationship between environment and behavior. An RBT can assist during Experimental Analysis, collect data during descriptive assessments, or provide information regarding the client.

Probing- asking a learner to perform a task we are unsure they can perform without providing assistance. an RBT can assist by probing new programs to confirm data collected during earlier assessments.

B-3. Assist with functional assessment procedures

Functional Assessments- determining cause and effect relationship between environment and behavior and altering either the antecedent or consequence or teaching a replacement behavior.

Functional (Experimental) Analysis- arranging antecedents and consequences so that their separate effect on a problem behavior can be observed and the function can be determined.

Descriptive Assessment- direct observation of behavior under naturally occurring conditions.

Indirect Assessment- using interviews, checklists, rating scales, and questionnaires to obtain information from people familiar with the learner.

C. SKILL ACQUISTION

C-1. Identify the essential components of a written skill acquisition plan.

1. Identify skill deficit.
2. Create a goal to address deficit.
3. Identify measurement procedures.
4. Assess current skill level (baseline).
5. Select and implement skill acquisition procedure(s).
6. Take data of target behaviors to determine effectiveness.
7. Modify if necessary to maintain/increase effectiveness.

C-2. Prepare for the session as required by the skill acquisition plan.

1. Determine what occurred last session to decide where to start.

2. Select skill acquisition procedures to complete during the session.

3. Prepare materials you will need for the skill acquisition procedure (including data collection materials).

C-3. Use contingencies of reinforcement.

- Unconditioned reinforcement
- Conditioned reinforcement
- Continuous reinforcement (CRF)
- Intermittent reinforcement (INT)
- Fixed Ratio (FR)
- Variable Ratio (VR)
- Fixed Interval (FI)
- Variable Interval (VI)

See Study Guide For More Details

C-4. Implement discrete-trial teaching procedures.

- Mass trial
- Distractor trial
- Random Rotation
- Expanded Trial
- Maintenance/Generalization

See Study Guide For More Details

C-5. Implement naturalistic teaching procedures.

Naturalistic teaching procedures are used to help learners generalize the skills they are learning through their ABA program. You are using the natural environment to

An example of implementing naturalistic teaching procedures would be to put a desirable item in clear view of a learner to encourage manding.

If a learner can identify and tact a picture of a dog, bringing them in the presence of a real dog and asking, "what is it?" would be another example.

C-6. Implement task analyzed chaining procedures.

Task analysis- breaking complex skills into smaller, teachable units creating sequential steps.

Forward Chaining- teach the first step of a task, then the second, then the third, until the entire sequence is mastered.

Backward Chaining- Complete a task entirely except for the last step. Teach the learner to complete the last step. Once they have mastered the last step, complete the whole task until the second-to-last step, and then allow them to master that. Continue this process until the entire task is learned.

C. SKILL ACQUISTION

C-7. Implement discrimination training.

Discrimination Training- Discrimination training is teaching a client how to tell the difference between two or more stimuli. Reinforcing occurrences of a behavior in the presence of one stimulus condition and not in the presence of another stimulus condition.

Simultaneous- both stimuli are presented at once.

Successive- only one stimulus condition is present.

C-8. Implement stimulus control transfer procedures.

Stimulus control transfer procedures are techniques in which prompts are discontinued once the target behavior is being displayed in the presence of the discriminative stimulus (Sd). Prompt fading and prompt delay are used in stimulus control transfer procedures.

Example:
RBT: "Say cup"
Learner: "Cup"
RBT: Points to a picture of a cup
Learner: "Cup"

C-9. Implement prompt and prompt fading procedures.

Prompt fading- there are two methods to fade a prompt.
- **Most to least-** With this method you start the most intrusive prompts and gradually fade to less intrusive prompts.
- **Least to most:** The method involves starting with the least intrusive prompts and moving up in the prompting hierarchy. This can be beneficial because it gives students to the opportunity to be independent and you are only providing as much prompting as needed. Once you introduce a task, allow wait time to see how they respond naturally. Then you can give a gestural prompt. If this doesn't produce a correct response, move up to a verbal, and so on.

C-10. Implement generalization and maintenance procedures.

Generalization- teach learned targets in the natural environment
  Examples:
  - teach the word car with many different pictures of different cars
  - having two people teach the same skill

Maintenance- including mastered item or skill into programs
  Examples:
  - discrete trials using random rotation or extended trials

C-11. Implement shaping procedures.

Shaping is the process of teaching a new behavior gradually by rewarding behaviors that progressively come close to the target behavior. Find an example of shaping on the Study Guide.

C-12. Implement token economy procedures.

A token economy is a system of generalized conditioned reinforcers.

The individual who receives the generalized tokens can save them and exchange for a variety of backup reinforcers.

Conditioned reinforcer- A stimulus that acquired its reinforcing value by being paired with other reinforcers.

Backup reinforcer- The reinforcer that is paired with a conditioned reinforcer or a generalized conditioned reinforcer.

D. BEHAVIOR REDUCTION

D-1. Identify essential components of a written behavior reduction plan.

A **behavior plan** is useful because it helps the behavior technician address behaviors effectively. Typically, the Behavior Analyst will develop the behavior plan and the RBT will implement it during ABA sessions.

A written behavior plan must include the following:
- Operational definitions of target behaviors
- Antecedent modifications
- Replacement behaviors
- Consequence modifications
- Persons responsible
- Emergency measures
- Function of behavior

D-2. Describe common functions of behavior.

The four functions of behavior are important to remember when providing ABA services. All behaviors are maintained by one or more of the four functions of behavior.

The four functions of behavior include:
- Attention
- Access to Tangibles
- Escape
- Automatic Reinforcement

D-3. Implement interventions based on modification of antecedents such as motivating operations and discriminative stimuli.

Motivating operations refers to a behavior concept which identifies the degree to which the learner will be reinforced by the consequences of their behavior.

An **establishing operation** increases the effectiveness of a reinforcer.

Discriminative stimuli, also known as SDs, are the stimuli that are used to elicit a specific response.

D-4. Implement differential reinforcement procedures.

DRI - Differential Reinforcement of Incompatible Behavior

DRA - Differential Reinforcement of Alternate Behavior

DRO - Differential Reinforcement of Other Behavior

DRL - Differential Reinforcement of Low Rates

D-5. Implement extinction procedures.

Extinction refers to the ABA principle of no longer providing reinforcement to a previously reinforced behavior. Basically, when the reinforcement for a behavior stops, the behavior will likely stop, as well.

Extinction involves no longer providing the reinforcement for a behavior. The reinforcement may have been attention in which case ignoring the behavior may be acceptable as an extinction procedure. However, when the reinforcement of the behavior is actually escape rather than attention, ignoring is not necessarily a true form of extinction. When a behavior is maintained by the function of escape, extinction would include no longer allowing escape from the demand.

D-6. Implement crisis/emergency procedures according to protocol.

The setting in which an RBT works will dictate what crisis or emergency procedures will be used in an ABA session. However, there are some general procedures that should be considered.

It is important to have a plan for how you as the RBT will address any maladaptive behaviors especially behaviors that could pose a danger to the client or anyone else. Typically, a supervisor or Behavior Analyst will be able to assist in developing this plan.

E. DOCUMENTATION and REPORTING

E-1. Effectively communicate with a supervisor in an ongoing manner.

- Taking an active role in effectively communicating all aspects of your daily interactions with your clients and caregivers
- Understanding boundaries in relation to your supervisor's time and responsibilities
- Knowing what situations should result in immediate or more urgent communication with your supervisor and knowing what situations can wait until your supervisor attends session for observation or has a meeting with you to discuss the case or client.
- Speaking respectfully and professionally.
- Accepting feedback and responding appropriately to feedback and communication from your supervisor.

E-2. Actively seek clinical direction from supervisor in a timely manner.

It is your responsibility as a Registered Behavior Technician to seek out guidance and direction from your supervisor(s) when needed. If you are unsure of protocol or steps you should be taking in a wide range of scenarios regarding your clients, you must contact a supervisor in a timely manner in order to achieve clear guidance before your next session (in most cases). You can, and should, request overlap sessions in which you can receive in-person supervision as well.

E-3. Report other variables that might affect the client in a timely manner.

There are many factors that an RBT or other ABA service provider should consider regarding a client's functioning. In the field of applied behavior analysis, setting events are sometimes neglected to be considered as influencers of behavior. Setting events are in a way broader experiences that a client may have.

Some examples of setting events include:
- Illness
- Lack of sleep
- Biological needs (like hunger)
- Changes in the client's home environment

E-4. Generate objective session notes for service verification by describing what occurred during the sessions, in accordance with applicable legal, regulatory, and workplace requirements.

It is important to complete session notes objectively and professionally. Objective refers to disclosing only facts and actual information or observations. This is in contrast to subjective information which includes adding your own personal thoughts and feelings into your session notes. When RBTs complete session notes, they should remember that the note will be included in that client's permanent record and therefore the note should be accurate and professionally written.

In a session note you could also mention the setting events or factors that may have influenced the client's behaviors throughout session. However, be sure to only use objective information and not to assume that you know why the child acted the way they did. For example, you may mention that the client's parent reported at the beginning of session that the client only slept five hours last night and that he had a fever last week.

Remember that it is important to generate objective session notes also so that others (such as other RBTs that may work with your client or your supervisor who oversees treatment planning) can be aware of what occurred during the session.

E-5. Comply with applicable legal, regulatory, and workplace data collection, storage, transportation, and documentation requirements.

There are laws and regulations regarding how to handle paperwork including data collection and documents specifically as it relates to how to store them and how to travel with them.

In the United States, you must comply with all HIPAA policies and regulations. HIPAA requires that a client's data and paperwork and identifying information be kept confidential and protected. You should store client data sheets, session notes, and paperwork in a secure location. You should always put them back after a session so that they are kept in that safe location.

F. PROFESSIONAL CONDUCT & SCOPE OF PRACTICE

F-1. Describe the BACB's RBT supervision requirements and the role of RBTs in the service-delivery system.

The RBT is required to provide the direct ABA service to the identified client including skill acquisition programs and behavior intervention plans.

The BACB presents a tiered service delivery model for the provision of behavior analysis services. In this model of service delivery, there are two possible organizational strategies. One includes multiple RBTs working under the direction of a BCBA or BCBA-D. The second one includes multiple RBTs working under the direction of a BCaBA while one or more BCaBAs can work under the direction of a BCBA or BCBA-D.

F-2. Respond appropriately to feedback and maintain or improve performance accordingly.

Responding appropriately to feedback and maintaining or improving performance accordingly is an important skill of RBTs. Part of an RBTs role includes taking feedback from a supervisor. The supervisor will be modifying treatment to help ensure the client is making progress on goals and to help with any behavioral concerns that arise.

To respond appropriately to feedback, the RBT should utilize active listening skills which involves listening to and comprehending what information the supervisor provides.

F-3. Communicate with stakeholders as authorized.

A Registered Behavior Technician's primary task is to implement ABA intervention as designed by their supervisor (typically a BCBA or BCaBA).

RBTs do not often provide formal communication with stakeholders. However, any communication that takes place must be respectful and professional in nature. Sometimes an RBT may participate in team meetings with the client's caregiver and sometimes other professionals, such as teachers or other service providers like speech therapists or occupational therapists.

F-4. Maintain professional boundaries.

It is essential to maintain professional boundaries in any human service position.

However, as an RBT, you may become attached to your client due to the intensity and involvement you have with the family.

However, it is important to always remember what your role is and that you are providing a professional service.

Do not develop any relationship outside the professional service provider – client relationship.

To avoid dual relationships or conflicts of interest, be sure to keep conversation to professional topics.

Do not speak very in depth about any personal issues (no more than enough to maintain a friendly, professional manner).

If you personally know a potential client, it is important to avoid working with that individual if possible.

Sometimes in rural communities, extra steps may be necessary to establish professional boundaries. Do not have contact with clients or their relatives on social media.

This is important to help maintain the professional boundaries of the service provider – client relationship.

F-5. Maintain client dignity.

Dignity refers to "the state or quality of being worthy of honor or respect." All people have the right to dignity and respect. Dignity is not something that people have to earn. You can maintain a client's dignity by showing respect at all times, maintaining privacy and confidentiality, and communicating effectively and professionally.

Maintaining professional boundaries and client dignity is an essential part of providing quality ABA services.

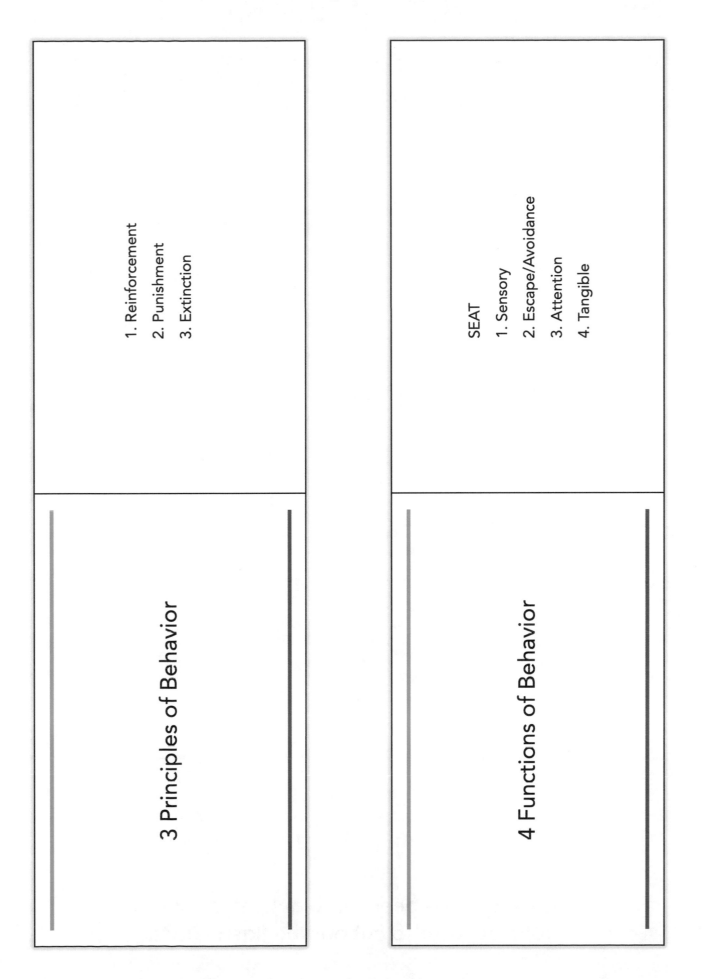

3 Principles of Behavior

1. Reinforcement
2. Punishment
3. Extinction

4 Functions of Behavior

SEAT

1. Sensory
2. Escape/Avoidance
3. Attention
4. Tangible

This page has been left blank intentionally
to allow user to cut out the flash cards.

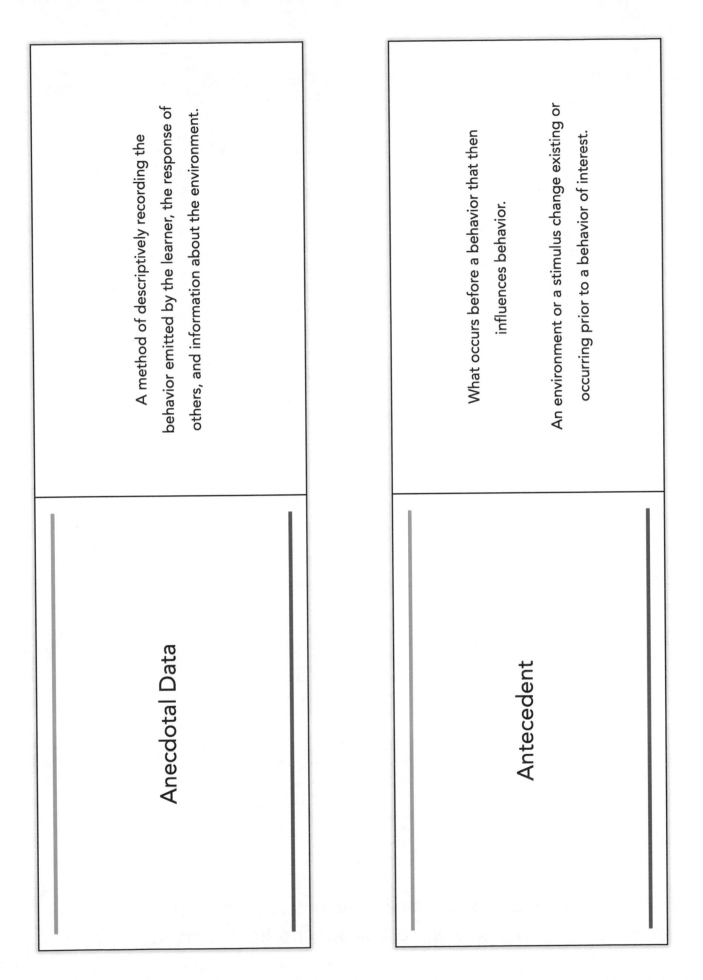

Anecdotal Data

A method of descriptively recording the behavior emitted by the learner, the response of others, and information about the environment.

Antecedent

What occurs before a behavior that then influences behavior.

An environment or a stimulus change existing or occurring prior to a behavior of interest.

This page has been left blank intentionally
to allow user to cut out the flash cards.

Applied Behavior Analysis

The science in which tactics derived from the principles of behavior are applied systematically to improve socially significant behavior and experimentation is used to identify the variables responsible for behavior change.

The scientific study of principles of learning and behavior.

How could you assist in training stakeholders?

RBT can assist with training stakeholders by giving them instruction, modeling, rehearsal, and feedback with regard to behavioral skills training.

This page has been left blank intentionally
to allow user to cut out the flash cards.

Attention Function

A function of behavior in which the individual is reinforced by receiving attention from others.

Automatic Reinforcement

(AKA self-stimming) The behavior itself is reinforcing and is not dependent on social interaction or receiving a tangible item.

This page has been left blank intentionally
to allow user to cut out the flash cards.

Backward Chaining

Training begins the link with the last behavior in the sequence.

Trainer performs all but the last step until the learner masters the last step.

Then trainer performs all but the lasts two steps until learner masters the last two steps and so on.

Baseline Data

Data taken before an intervention takes place.

Describes the existing level of performance.

This page has been left blank intentionally
to allow user to cut out the flash cards.

Chaining

A specific sequence of discrete responses, each associated with a particular stimulus condition.

When components are linked together, they form a chain that produces a terminal outcome.

Components of a Written Behavior Plan

1. Identify, describe, create a goal for a behavior in observable terms.

2. Assess antecedent/consequence that may maintain behavior.

3. Identify hypothesis of function of behavior.

4. Identify possible replacement behaviors.

5. Select and implement antecedent/consequence based interventions.

6. Create crisis intervention plan.

7. Implementation, modification, generalization and maintenance procedures.

This page has been left blank intentionally
to allow user to cut out the flash cards.

Conditioned Response

A behavior that does not come naturally, but must be learned by the individual by pairing a neutral stimulus with an unconditioned stimulus.

Conditioned Stimulus

A previously neutral stimulus that, after repeated association with an unconditioned stimulus, elicits the response produced by the unconditioned stimulus itself.

This page has been left blank intentionally
to allow user to cut out the flash cards.

Consequence

Events that follow behavior and may influence it including increasing or decreasing it in the future.

May be reinforcers or punishers.

Contingency

Refers to and if_____, then_____ relationship between a behavior and a consequence.

This page has been left blank intentionally
to allow user to cut out the flash cards.

Continuous Reinforcement Schedule

Providing reinforcement each time the behavior/response occurs.

Differential Reinforcement

Reinforcing one response class and withholding reinforcement from another response class.

Behavior receiving reinforcement should increase while the behavior for which reinforcement is being withheld should decrease.

This page has been left blank intentionally
to allow user to cut out the flash cards.

Differential Reinforcement of Alternative Behaviors (DRA)

Focus on increasing a desirable alternative behavior that directly or indirectly interferes with the performance of the undesired target behavior.

(i.e. reinforce knitting or giving a self manicure instead of biting nails; reinforce appropriate language instead of punishing swearing at others)

Differential Reinforcement of Incompatible Behaviors (DRI)

Similar to DRA but you choose and alternative behavior to reinforce that, if performed, would be incompatible with the undesired target behavior.

(i.e. playing nicely vs. fighting; on task behavior vs. off task behavior; in seat vs. out of seat; deep breathing vs. yelling)

This page has been left blank intentionally
to allow user to cut out the flash cards.

Differential Reinforcement of Low Rates (DRL)

Entails reinforcing for reductions in the frequency of the undesired behavior.

Often used when individual is engaging in a behavior too frequently.

Differential Reinforcement of Other Behaviors (DRO)

Providing a reinforcer after a particular time frame without the target behavior.

For example engaging in any other behavior except the target behavior.

(i.e. every 5 minutes without hitting, individual receives a sticker)

This page has been left blank intentionally
to allow user to cut out the flash cards.

Direct Observation Preference Assessment

Identify what is motivating the individual.

The more time spent with an item, the stronger the presumed preference.

Discrete Trial Training

Structured instructional methodology used to teach new behaviors

Designed to maximize a learner's potential by presenting information in a three-part teaching unit.

Based on Antecedent - Behavior - Consequence format.

A - B - C (Stimulus - Response - Consequence)

Main objective is to teach children how to learn from their natural environment and make learning reinforcing.

This page has been left blank intentionally
to allow user to cut out the flash cards.

Discrimination Training

Procedure to teach between two targets.

Trial training using phases.

(i.e. phases 1 - 6 Mass Trials of target, Block Trials, and Random Rotation)

Discriminative Stimulus (SD)

Environmental cue or instruction that signals that reinforcement is available for a target behavior.

This page has been left blank intentionally
to allow user to cut out the flash cards.

Data that is a calculation of the amount of time a behavior occurs.

The amount of time a response is performed.

Track from onset to offset.

Typically used for behaviors that last too long or too short. (i.e. on task behavior, social interactions, engaging in stereotypy)

Duration Data

A type of verbal operant that occurs when a speaker repeats the verbal behavior of another speaker.

Occurs in response to other verbal behavior.

Listener is "echoing" what they hear.

Echoic

This page has been left blank intentionally
to allow user to cut out the flash cards.

Teaching procedures that are designed in such a way that the learning does not have to - and does not - make mistakes as she or he learns new information or procedures.

DTT is Errorless Learning.

Errorless Learning

A function of behavior to escape or avoid having to do something.

Escape/Avoidance Function

This page has been left blank intentionally
to allow user to cut out the flash cards.

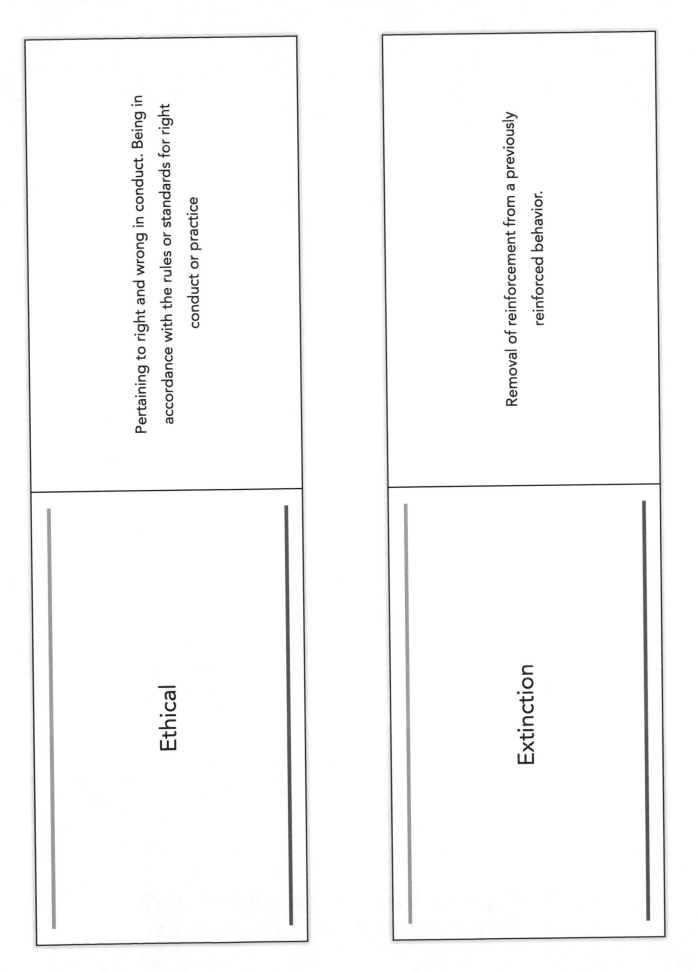

Pertaining to right and wrong in conduct. Being in accordance with the rules or standards for right conduct or practice

Ethical

Removal of reinforcement from a previously reinforced behavior.

Extinction

This page has been left blank intentionally
to allow user to cut out the flash cards.

Prior to the behavior decreasing you will see a temporary increase in behavior.

Immediate increase in frequency in responding.

Extinction Burst

The first correct response is rewarded only after a specified amount of time has elapsed.

Fixed Interval
Reinforcement Schedule

This page has been left blank intentionally
to allow user to cut out the flash cards.

Fixed Ratio
Reinforcement Schedule

Reinforcement should be delivered after a constant or "fixed" number of responses.

Forward Chaining

Training begins the link with the first behavior in the sequence.

Training only occurs on the steps currently mastered and current step (no training on steps after that).

This page has been left blank intentionally
to allow user to cut out the flash cards.

Frequency Data

A form of continuous measurement.

Data in which you tally each time the behavior occurs.

Typically used for behaviors with discrete beginning and ending points.

Typically used for behaviors with discrete beginning and ending points. (i.e. throwing items, going to the gym, taking medicine, hitting another person)

Most frequently used type of data collection.

Function

The purpose or meaning behind a behavior.

This page has been left blank intentionally
to allow user to cut out the flash cards.

Functional Behavior Assessment (FBA)

Putting one or more Functional Analysis together.

Can consist of:

- Direct observation

- Interview

- Functional analysis (experimental)

- File Review

In an FBA behavior plans must include replacement skills.

Generalization

When the effort of reinforcement is extended beyond the conditions in which the training has taken place or to behaviors other than those included in training.

This page has been left blank intentionally
to allow user to cut out the flash cards.

Generalized Conditioned Reinforcers

Stimuli that have been paired with a variety of unconditioned and conditioned reinforcers. (i.e. praise, attention, money, tokens)

Graphing

Graphing is a method of representing data in a visual way so that we can se patterns and direction over time.

- Line Graph (most common) shows patterns, trends
  - Bar Graph shows portions of a whole
  - Pie Chart shows portions of a whole

This page has been left blank intentionally
to allow user to cut out the flash cards.

How to Prepare for Data Collection

1. Read data from last session

2. Prepare material and programs for current session based on data from last session.

3. Determine what programs you plan to work on during the session.

4. Gather materials for those programs.

5. Set up the first set of programs so they are ready for the client when you begin your session.

Intermittent Reinforcement Schedule

Reinforcement is delivered after only SOME of the desired responses occur.

This page has been left blank intentionally
to allow user to cut out the flash cards.

Mand

Short for demand, command or reprimand.

A type of verbal operant in which a speaker asks for (or states, demands, implies, etc.) what he needs or wants.

Only type of verbal operant that directly benefits the speaker b/c the mand allows the speaker to receive reinforcers.

Momentary Time Sampling

Look up at the client immediately at pre-designated points and record whether the behavior occurred at that precise moment.

Example: presence or absence of client's stereotypic behavior (stimming).

This page has been left blank intentionally
to allow user to cut out the flash cards.

Multiple Stimuli Without Replacement Preference Assessment

Chosen item is removed from the array, the order or replacement of the remaining items is rearranged, and the next trial begins with a reduced number of items in the array.

Multiple Stimuli With Replacement Preference Assessment

Item chosen by the learner remains in the array and all other items that were not selected are replaced with new ones.

This page has been left blank intentionally
to allow user to cut out the flash cards.

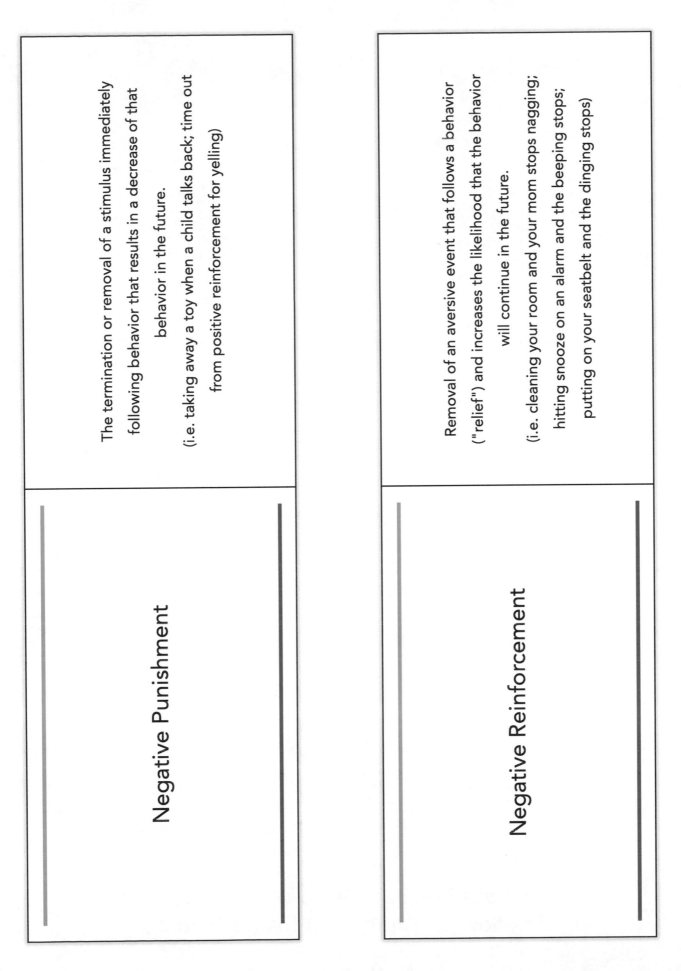

Negative Punishment

The termination or removal of a stimulus immediately following behavior that results in a decrease of that behavior in the future.

(i.e. taking away a toy when a child talks back; time out from positive reinforcement for yelling)

Negative Reinforcement

Removal of an aversive event that follows a behavior ("relief") and increases the likelihood that the behavior will continue in the future.

(i.e. cleaning your room and your mom stops nagging; hitting snooze on an alarm and the beeping stops; putting on your seatbelt and the dinging stops)

This page has been left blank intentionally
to allow user to cut out the flash cards.

Operant Behavior

Behavior that is controlled or influenced by consequences.

Behavior whose future frequency is determined by a history of consequences.

Operant Conditioning

A type of learning where behavior is controlled by consequences.

Behavior followed by pleasant consequences tends to be repeated.

Behavior followed by unpleasant consequences tends not to be repeated.

This page has been left blank intentionally
to allow user to cut out the flash cards.

What does the behavior look like, what happens exactly,
what does it sound like?

Operational Definition

A type of measurement used when the behavior you are
assessing results in a lasting product or outcome.

Example: number of written assignments completed

Permanent Product
Recording Procedures

This page has been left blank intentionally
to allow user to cut out the flash cards.

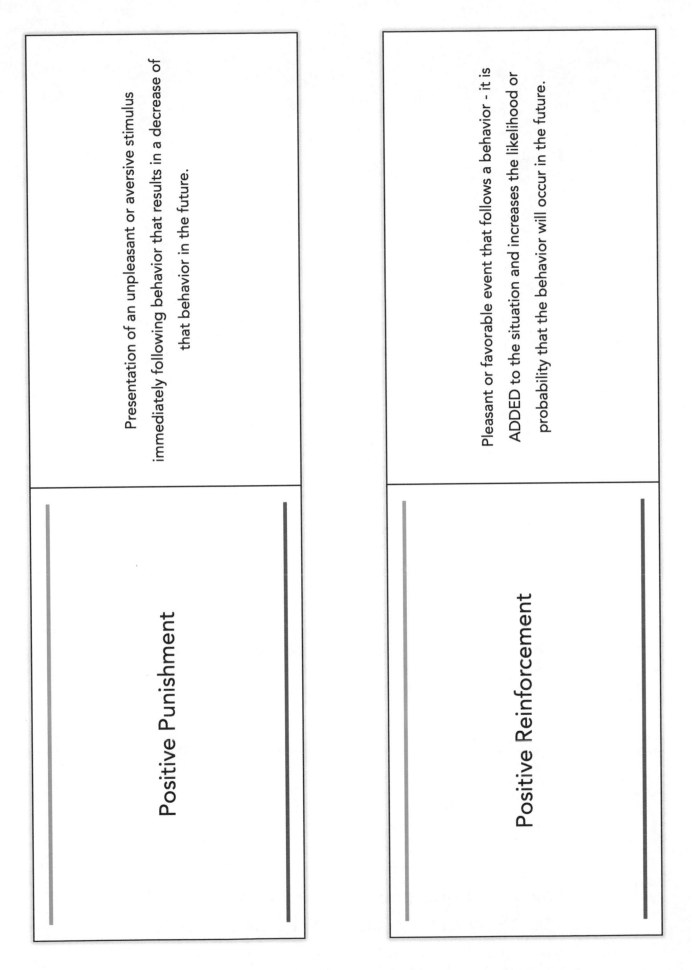

Positive Punishment

Presentation of an unpleasant or aversive stimulus immediately following behavior that results in a decrease of that behavior in the future.

Positive Reinforcement

Pleasant or favorable event that follows a behavior - it is ADDED to the situation and increases the likelihood or probability that the behavior will occur in the future.

This page has been left blank intentionally
to allow user to cut out the flash cards.

Preference Assessment

Aims to identify an individual's favorite things so that they can be used as rewards or potential "reinforcers" for desired behavior.

How to Prepare for Skill Acquisition Plan

1. Determine what occurred last session to decide where to start.

2. Select skill acquisition procedures to complete during session.

3. Prepare materials you will need for the skill acquisition (including data collection protocols).

This page has been left blank intentionally
to allow user to cut out the flash cards.

Professional Boundaries

Avoid dual relationships, conflicts of interest, social media contacts. Always take notes.

Prompt

Specific antecedent that directly facilitates performance of behavior.

Assistance provided to engage in desired behavior or response.

This page has been left blank intentionally
to allow user to cut out the flash cards.

Prompt Fading

The gradual elimination of a stimulus prompt as the behavior continues to occur in the presence of the SD.

Prompt Hierarchy

The so called "pyramid" of the various levels of prompting.

We need to establish a hierarchy of prompts from the least to most or most to least intrusive for each instructional task.

This page has been left blank intentionally
to allow user to cut out the flash cards.

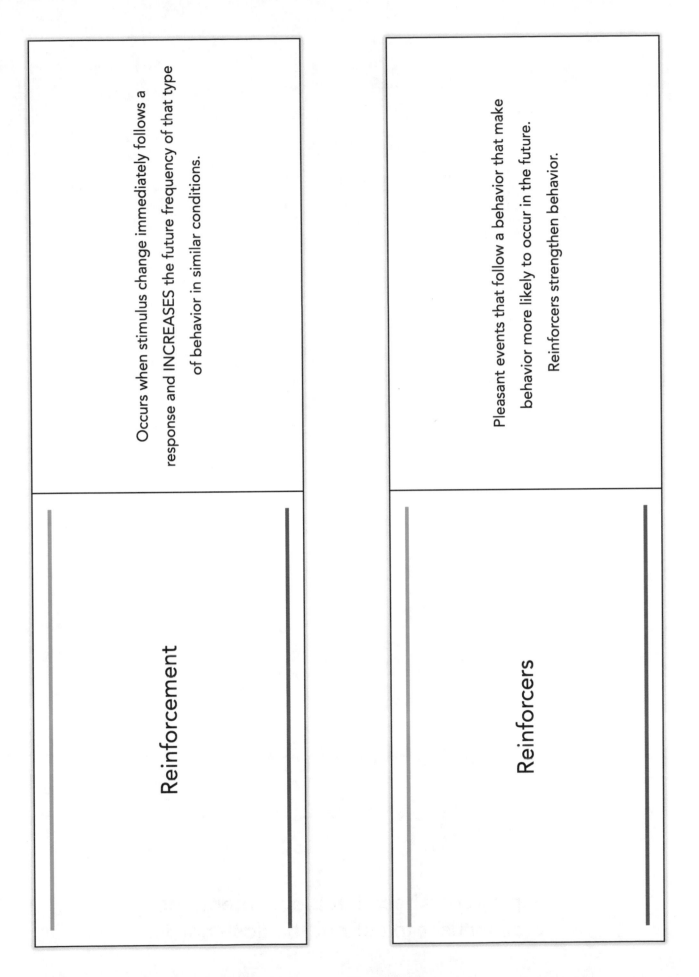

Reinforcement

Occurs when stimulus change immediately follows a response and INCREASES the future frequency of that type of behavior in similar conditions.

Reinforcers

Pleasant events that follow a behavior that make behavior more likely to occur in the future. Reinforcers strengthen behavior.

This page has been left blank intentionally
to allow user to cut out the flash cards.

A process by which one systematically and differentially reinforces successive approximations to a terminal behavior.

Shaping

Exaggerate some physical dimension of the relevant stimulus to help the individual respond correctly.
Prompt is within the stimulus itself.
Can be used for color or size determination.

Stimulus Fading

This page has been left blank intentionally
to allow user to cut out the flash cards.

Stimulus Generalization

Generalization or transfer of a response to situations other than those in which the training takes place.

Across people: The learner's ability to respond to people other than those involved in the original teaching

Across environments: The learner's ability to respond in different locations other than the "table and chair"

Tact

Short for contact.
A type of verbal operant in which speaker names things and actions that the speaker had direct contact with through any of the sense modes.

This page has been left blank intentionally
to allow user to cut out the flash cards.

Tangible Function

A function of behavior in which the individual wants to obtain a tangible item.

The individual wants a preferred item or activity.

Task Analysis

Involves breaking a complex skill into smaller, teachable units, the product of which is a series of sequentially ordered steps or tasks.

This page has been left blank intentionally
to allow user to cut out the flash cards.

Reinforcement systems in which tokens are earned for a variety of behaviors and are used to purchase or exchange for a variety of backup reinforcers such as food, activities, trips, toys.

Token Economies

Process by which prompts are removed once the target behavior is occurring in the presence of the SD.

Transfer of Stimulus Control

This page has been left blank intentionally
to allow user to cut out the flash cards.

A behavior that occurs naturally due to a given stimulus.

i.e. Dogs salivating in the presence of food; yelping upon being bitten by an insect.

Unconditioned Response

A stimulus that elicits an unconditioned response.

i.e. Food is an unconditioned stimulus for a hungry animal and salivation is the unconditioned response.

Unconditioned Stimulus

This page has been left blank intentionally
to allow user to cut out the flash cards.

Variable Interval
Reinforcement Schedule

Where a response is rewarded after an unpredictable (variable) amount of time has elapsed.

Variable Ratio
Reinforcement Schedule

Reinforcement is provided after an unpredictable (variable) number of responses.

This schedule is the most resistant to extinction.

This page has been left blank intentionally
to allow user to cut out the flash cards.

Verbal Behavior

Behavior that is reinforced through the mediation of another person's behavior.

Involves a social interaction between speakers and listeners.

Listener reinforces the speaker.

Whole Interval Recording

Did the behavior occur for the <u>whole</u> interval that you are looking for it?

Underestimates the behavior.

Example: the total time devoted to remaining on task.

This page has been left blank intentionally
to allow user to cut out the flash cards.

Made in the USA
Columbia, SC
30 March 2024

33791931R00072